Pussy Cat

and

Morag Styles

Illustrated by
Penelope Taylor

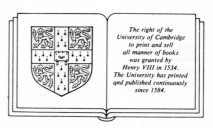

The right of the
University of Cambridge
to print and sell
all manner of books
was granted by
Henry VIII in 1534.
The University has printed
and published continuously
since 1584.

Cambridge University Press

Cambridge
New York   Port Chester
Melbourne   Sydney

Published by the Press Syndicate of the University of Cambridge
The Pitt Building, Trumpington Street, Cambridge CB2 1RP
40 West 20th Street, New York, NY 10011-4211, USA
10 Stamford Road, Oakleigh, Melbourne 3166, Australia

Project editor Claire Llewellyn

First published 1991

Printed in Great Britain at the University Press, Cambridge

British Library cataloguing in publication data
Pussy cat, pussy cat.
1. Poetry in English – Anthologies
I. Cook, Helen 1954–   II. Styles, Morag
821.008

ISBN 0 521 39946 7

Acknowledgements

'Pussy Cat, Pussy Cat' by Spike Milligan from *Startling Verse for All the Family*, Puffin Books, © Spike Milligan Productions; 'Fluffy' by Edwin Thumboo from *Child's Delight*, Federal Publishers Singapore, 1972 © Edwin Thumboo; 'If You, Like Me . . .' from *Dogs and Dragons, Trees and Dreams* by Karla Kuskin. 'If You, Like Me' originally appeared in *Any Me I Want to Be* by Karla Kuskin. Copyright © 1972 by Karla Kuskin; 'Cat' from *And I Dance* by Keith Bosley, reproduced by kind permission of Angus & Robertson Publishers; 'Poem' from *Collected Poems of William Carlos Williams, 1909–1939, vol I*, copyright 1938 by New Directions Publishing Corp., reprinted by permission of New Directions Publishing Corp and Carcanet Press Ltd; 'Why Did You Go?' from *Complete Poems 1913–1962* by E. E. Cummings, reprinted by permission of Granada Books, part of HarperCollins Publishers – 'Why Did You Go' is also reprinted from *Tulips and Chimneys* by E. E. Cummings, edited by George James Firmage, by permission of Liveright Publishing Corporation. Copyright 1923, 1925 and renewed 1951, 1953 by E. E. Cummings. Copyright © 1973, 1976 by the Trustees for the E. E. Cummings Trust. Copyright © 1973, 1976 by George James Firmage; 'A Kitten' by Eleanor Farjeon from *Invitation to a Mouse*, Hodder and Stoughton 1986; 'Cat' from *Small Poems* by Valerie Worth, poems copyright © 1972 by Valerie Worth, reprinted by permission of Farrar, Straus & Giroux, Inc; 'On a Night of Snow' by Elizabeth Coatsworth from *Night and the Cat*, Macmillan Publishing Co, by permission of Margaret Beston; extract from 'Hunting with Henry the Cat' by Mick Gowar, from *Third Time Lucky* by Mick Gowar (Viking Kestrel, 1988) copyright © Mick Gowar, 1988; 'Granny Tom' by Kit Wright, from *Cat Among the Pigeons* by Kit Wright (Viking Kestrel, 1988), copyright © Kit Wright, 1988; 'Fat Cat' by Ann Bonner by permission of the author; 'Bring Back the Cat' by Roger McGough, reprinted by permission of the Peters Fraser & Dunlop Group Ltd; 'The Singing Cat' by Stevie Smith from *Collected Poems*, Penguin Books Ltd, by permission of James MacGibbon; 'Uncle Paul of Pimlico' by Mervyn Peake from *Rhymes Without Reason*, Methuen Children's Books, © 1974 Maeve Peake; 'The Greater Cats' by Vita Sackville-West © Nigel Nicolson; 'Tiger' from *Small Poems Again* by Valerie Worth, poems copyright © 1975, 1986 by Valerie Worth, reprinted by permission of Farrar, Straus & Giroux, Inc; extract from 'India' from *Selected Poems of W J Turner*, Oxford University Press, 1939; 'There are Times' from *700 Chinese Proverbs*, collected and translated by Henry Hart, © Stanford University Press; 'Roar' by Karla Kuskin from *Roar and More*. Copyright © 1956 by Karla Kuskin.

Every effort has been made to reach copyright holders; the publishers would be glad to hear from anyone whose rights they have unknowingly infringed.

Contents

Pussy Cat, Pussy Cat

Pussy cat, pussy cat, where have you been?
I've been up to London to look at the queen.
Pussy cat, pussy cat, what did you there?
I frightened a little mouse under her chair.

Traditional

Pussy Cat, Pussy Cat

Pussy cat, pussy cat,
Where have you been?
I went to London
To see the queen.
Pussy cat, pussy cat,
What did you see?
I saw a policeman
Following me.
Pussy cat, pussy cat,
What did he do?
He said to me,
'Home you go!
Shoo, shoo, shoo!'

Spike Milligan

5

Fluffy

Tit for tat,
Catch a rat.

I have soft paws,
I purr and mew
I have sharp claws,
But not for you.

Tit for tat,
Catch a rat.

Edwin Thumboo

Who am I?

I am a cat
purring
in my sleeping box
in the kitchen.

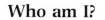

I am a cat
scratching
at the table
sharpening my claws.

I am a cat
eating
nine lives gourmet.

Ian (aged 7)

If You . . .

If you,
Like me,
Were made of fur
And sun warmed you,
Like me,
You'd purr.

Karla Kuskin

Cat

Cat
purring

four furry paws
walking

delicate-
ly
     between
flower stems
stalking

butter-
flies

Keith Bosley

Poem

As the cat
climbed over
the top of

the jamcloset
first the right
forefoot

carefully
then the hind
stepped down

into the pit of
the empty
flowerpot

William Carlos Williams

Why Did You Go?

why did you go
little four paws?
you forgot to shut
your big eyes.

where did you go?
like little kittens
are all the leaves
which open in the rain

little kittens who
are called spring,
is what we stroke
maybe asleep.

do you know? or maybe did
something go away
ever so quietly
when we weren't looking

e e cummings

A Kitten

He's nothing much but fur
And two round eyes of blue,
He has a giant purr
And a midget mew.

He darts and pats the air,
He starts and pricks his ear,
When there is nothing there
For him to see and hear.

He runs around in rings,
But why we cannot tell;
With sideways leaps he springs
At things invisible –

Then half-way through a leap
His startled eyeballs close,
And he drops off to sleep
With one paw on his nose.

Eleanor Farjeon

Cat

The spotted cat hops
Up to a white radiator-cover
As warm as summer, and there,

Between pots of green leaves growing,
By a window of cold panes showing
Silver of snow thin across the grass,

She settles slight neat muscles
Smoothly down within
Her comfortable fur,

Slips in the ends, front paws,
Tail, until she is readied,
Arranged, shaped for sleep.

Valerie Worth

The Cat

Creeping by night,
Creeping by night,
Creeping by night,
   Quoth the grey cat;
Creeping by night,
With neither star nor gleam,
Nor brightness nor light,
   Quoth the grey cat!

Traditional, Gaelic

On a Night of Snow

Cat, if you go out-doors you must walk in the snow,
You will come back with little white shoes on your feet,
Little white slippers of snow that have heels of sleet.
Stay by the fire, my Cat. Lie still, do not go.
See how the flames are leaping and hissing low,
I will bring you a saucer of milk like a marguerite,
So white and so smooth, so spherical and so sweet –
Stay with me, Cat. Out-doors the wild winds blow.

Out-doors the wild winds blow, Mistress, and dark is the night.
Strange voices cry in the trees, intoning strange lore
And more than cats move, lit by our eyes' green light,
On silent feet where the meadow grasses hang hoar –
Mistress, there are portents abroad of magic and might,
And things that are yet to be done. Open the door!

Elizabeth Coatsworth

EXTRACT FROM
Hunting with Henry the Cat

Small black-and-white cat –
white face white tummy white paws
sharp eyes sharp ears and
. . . very sharp claws

stretches out along the floor
scratches round his bowl, then

out of the door to the garden.

(But don't be fooled by his
slow and sleepy, easy walk – he's going
        hunting!)

A sunny path,
      he's lying with his front feet in
          the air.
(He's very, very still,
he's *not* asleep . . .)

SNAP!

He's missed . . . a butterfly

Two wings of creamy-white
like fluttering crisps

(A snack that got away –
to flutter back another day?)

Rolls over, up and
prowling now – a Tiger in a Forest of
Chrysanthemums . . .

he's *hunting* – yes, but *what?*
Caterpillars? . . . Centipedes?

(Anything That Moves, says Henry.)

Mick Gowar

19

Granny Tom

There's a cat among the pigeons
In the yard, in the yard,
And it seems he isn't trying
Very hard.
Should a pigeon chance to swoop,
You can see his whiskers droop
And his tail not twitch its loop
In the yard.

For the cat is growing old
In the yard, in the yard,
And the pigeons leave him cold.
He has starred
In his youth in many chases,
When he put them through their paces.
Now he knows just what his place is
In the yard.

He's a snoozer in the sun
And his hunting days are done.
He's a dozer by the wall
And he pounces not at all
For he knows he no more can. He
Might well be the pigeons' *granny*
In the yard!

Kit Wright

Fat Cat

I have such a fat
cat.
A greedy cat.
A lazy cat.

When bees are busy
and hot sun
shines
fat cat sleeps.

Lazy cat yawns.
Comes downstairs.
Mews
for her tea.

Greedy cat's belly,
full.
She sits in the garden's
shadow.
Watches martins
make circles
in the sky.

Yellow moon rises.
First star
Shines.
She's a wide-awake cat.
Not-so-fat-cat.
Gone for the night cat.
Goodbye.

Ann Bonner

Bring Back the Cat

Bring back the cat
Bring back the cat
My little girl say
Bring back the cat

Bring back the cat
Bring back the cat
My little girl
She really like that

My little girl she four in May
Got a pet kitten, it black and grey
Playing in the garden just the other day
Kitten went missing, must have gone astray
(Unless some kittennapper took her away)

Went right down to the RSPCA
Told me not to worry, it would be OK
Nothing more to do 'cept hope and pray
Maybe he bring it back some day
That why my little girl she say:

Bring back the cat
Bring back the cat
My little girl say
Bring back the cat

Bring back the cat
Bring back the cat
My little girl she
Really like that

Roger McGough

The Singing Cat

It was a little captive cat
Up in a crowded train
His mistress takes him from his box
To ease his fretful pain.

She holds him tight upon her knee
The graceful animal
And all the people look at him
He is so beautiful.

But oh he pricks and oh he prods
And turns upon her knee
Then lifteth up his innocent voice
In plaintive melody.

He lifteth up his innocent voice
He lifteth up, he singeth
And to each human countenance
A smile of grace he bringeth.

He lifteth up his innocent paw
Upon her breast he clingeth
And everybody cries, Behold
The cat, the cat that singeth.

He lifteth up his innocent voice
He lifteth up, he singeth
And all the people warm themselves
In the love his beauty bringeth.

Stevie Smith

Uncle Paul of Pimlico

My Uncle Paul of Pimlico
Has seven cats as white as snow,
Who sit at his enormous feet
And watch him, as a special treat,
Play the piano upside down,
In his delightful dressing gown;
The firelight leaps, the parlour glows,
And, while the music ebbs and flows,
They smile (while purring the refrains),
At little thoughts that cross their brains.

Mervyn Peake

The Greater Cats

The greater cats with golden eyes
Stare out between the bars.
Deserts are there, and different skies,
And night with different stars.

Vita Sackville-West

Tiger

The tiger
Has swallowed
A black sun,

In his cold
Cage he
Carries it still:

Black flames
Flicker through
His fur,

Black rays soar
From the centres
Of his eyes.

Valerie Worth

EXTRACT FROM **India**

They hunt, the velvet tigers in the jungle,
The spotted jungle full of shapeless patches –
Sometimes they're leaves, sometimes they're hanging flowers,
Sometimes they're hot gold patches of the sun:
They hunt, the velvet tigers in the jungle!

W J Turner

There are Times

There are times when even
the tiger sleeps.

Chinese proverb

Roar

This is a tiger
Striped with black
You snarl at him
And he'll snarl back

SSNNAAARRRLLL

Karla Kuskin

Tiger, Tiger

Tiger, tiger, you scare me
With your coat soft and fair.
I do not dare
Go too near.

But when you are in a cage
I don't care.

You have sharp eyes,
Not like mine,
And sharp nails,
I bite mine.
Worst of all
Those big white teeth
Could eat me in one huge bite.

Sarah Harris (aged 8)

31

EXTRACT FROM **The Tyger**

Tyger Tyger, burning bright,
In the forests of the night;
What immortal hand or eye,
Could frame thy fearful symmetry?

William Blake